THE BRIDGE AT SELMA

Turning Points in American History

THE BRIDGE AT SELMA

Marilyn Miller

Silver Burdett Company, Morristown, New Jersey

Cincinnati; Glenview, Ill.; San Carlos, Calif.;
Dallas; Atlanta; Agincourt, Ontario

Acknowledgements

We would like to thank the following people for reviewing the manuscript and for their guidance and helpful suggestions: Professor Kenneth Kusmer, Department of History, Temple University; and Diane Sielski, Library Media Coordinator, Coldwater Village Exempted Schools, Coldwater, Ohio.

Cover photo courtesy of Laurance G. Henry/Schomburg Center (NYPL)
Title-page photo courtesy of Matt Herron/Black Star
Contents-page photo courtesy of Bob Fletcher
Calhoun portrait on p. 22 courtesy of the National Portrait Gallery
Wallace photo on p. 23 courtesy of UPI/Bettmann Archive
Gandhi photo on p. 42 courtesy of UPI/Bettmann Archive

Library of Congress Cataloging in Publication Data

Miller, Marilyn, 1946–
   The bridge at Selma.

   (Turning points in American history)
   "Created by Media Projects, Inc."—T.p. verso.
   Bibliography: p.
   Includes index.
   Summary: Describes the far-reaching repercussions of the events of March 7, 1965 when 525 men, women, and children in Alabama attempted to march from Selma to the state capitol in Montgomery in order to register to vote.
      1. Selma (Ala.)—Race relations—Juvenile literature.
   2. Selma (Ala.)—Riot, 1965—Juvenile literature.

   3. Afro-Americans—Civil rights—Juvenile literature.
   [1. Selma (Ala.)—Riot, 1965. 2. Afro-Americans—Civil rights. 3. Civil rights—History. 4. Race relations]
   I. Media Projects Incorporated. II. Title. III. Series.
   F334.S4M55 1985 976.1'45 84-40379
   ISBN 0-382-06826-2

 Created by Media Projects, Inc.

Series design by Bruce Glassman
Ellen Coffey, Project Manager
Frank L. Kurtz, Project Editor
Jeffrey Woldt, Photo Research Editor

Copyright © 1985 Silver Burdett Company

Published simultaneously in Canada by GLC/Silver Burdett Publishers

Manufactured in the United States of America

CONTENTS

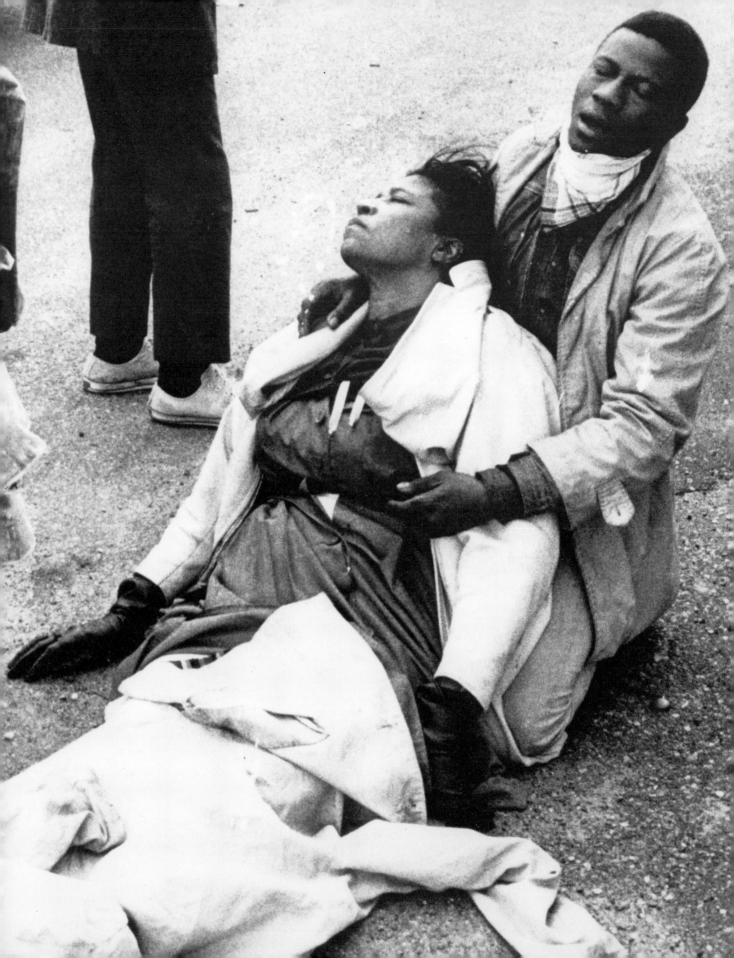

INTRODUCTION

BLOODY SUNDAY

On the surface, March 7, 1965, seemed like any other late-winter Sunday in Selma, Alabama. Purple-blue clouds hid the sun over this small Southern city of 28,000. A chill wind cut into the faces of those deciding to brave the weather. Still, the downtown shopping district was crowded. At the Selma Country Club, some members played bridge while others watched TV. At the Echo Bowling Alley, teenagers took up all ten lanes. Business was brisk at the Selmont Drive-In.

But in another part of the city, a different kind of activity was taking place. Before the end of the day, the events that occurred there would appear on TV screens across the country. Because of these

Roadside, Selma; March 7, 1965

events, Monday's newspapers would carry the word "Selma" in bold headlines.

The Selma pictured in these newspaper stories was not the city of comfortable homes that almost half its residents lived in. It was not the Selma composed of mansions that the city's wealthiest citizens called home.

The Selma in these stories was composed of white clapboard shanties and red-brick housing projects. In this Selma lived the more than 15,000 blacks who made up more than half of its population.

Early in the afternoon of March 7, groups of these blacks were streaming out of Brown's Chapel Methodist Church. Brown's was located in the heart of the black community. During the past two months, the church had been the nerve

7

center of a drive to gain voting rights for Selma's blacks.

The Fifteenth Amendment to the Constitution, passed in 1870, stated that the right to vote could not be denied on the basis of race. Yet in Selma in 1965, only 156 blacks of voting age were registered. This situation was typical of a number of states in the Deep South. Using a variety of tactics—some legal, some not—whites had kept blacks from voting.

Since January, blacks had been marching in groups to the Dallas County courthouse in an attempt to register to vote. So far, not a single black had succeeded. Sunday, March 7, was another day to try.

This time, the destination was the state capitol, in Montgomery, located about fifty miles east of Selma. Some 525 men, women, and children were going there to protest the lack of voting rights to Governor George C. Wallace. Governor Wallace

John Lewis, of the Student Nonviolent Coordinating Committee

had banned the march, and the marchers were afraid that state troopers would try to stop them, as had already happened in other parts of Alabama. The day before, those planning to march had practiced defending themselves against tear gas. Now nothing remained but to wait until Hosea Williams and John Lewis, leaders of the march, gave the signal to start.

Hosea Williams was an aide to the Reverend Dr. Martin Luther King, Jr., leader of the Southern Christian Leadership Conference (SCLC) and one of the chief organizers of the voting-rights drive in Selma. King's associates had persuaded him not to lead them on March 7, because of a series of death threats against him, and Williams was to take his place. John Lewis, the other leader, was the chairman of the Student Nonviolent Coordinating Committee (SNCC, pronounced "Snick"). Together these organizations had mounted the voting-rights campaign.

In small groups, the marchers left the chapel. On their backs they carried bedrolls and packs. Four ambulances trailed behind them. The first objective was the Edmund Pettus Bridge, more than three quarters of a mile away. The bridge formed part of Highway 80, which led to Mont-gomery. Three hundred yards away from the bridge, the marchers passed three dozen state troopers standing in the shadow of the Selma Times-Journal building. The troopers made no move to interrupt the march.

The marchers could see the dingy brown bridge as they approached, but they could not yet see over the rise to the other side. Slowly, they continued on. The atmosphere seemed still, except for the sound of the rushing wind and of the marchers' footsteps. Then the first marchers saw what awaited them.

More than fifty state troopers were massed about two hundred yards beyond the bridge. The troopers were armed with clubs and whips, and they had gas-mask pouches slung across their shoulders. In their uniforms and helmets, they looked like a blue picket fence stretching across the highway. Behind them, three dozen possemen loomed menacingly. Fifteen of them were on horseback. The possemen were volunteers engaged by the Dallas County sheriff, Jim Clark. The sheriff was well known as a militant racist. At the moment, he was sitting in a nearby car with the state's director of public safety, Colonel Al Lingo. Both men believed in using force

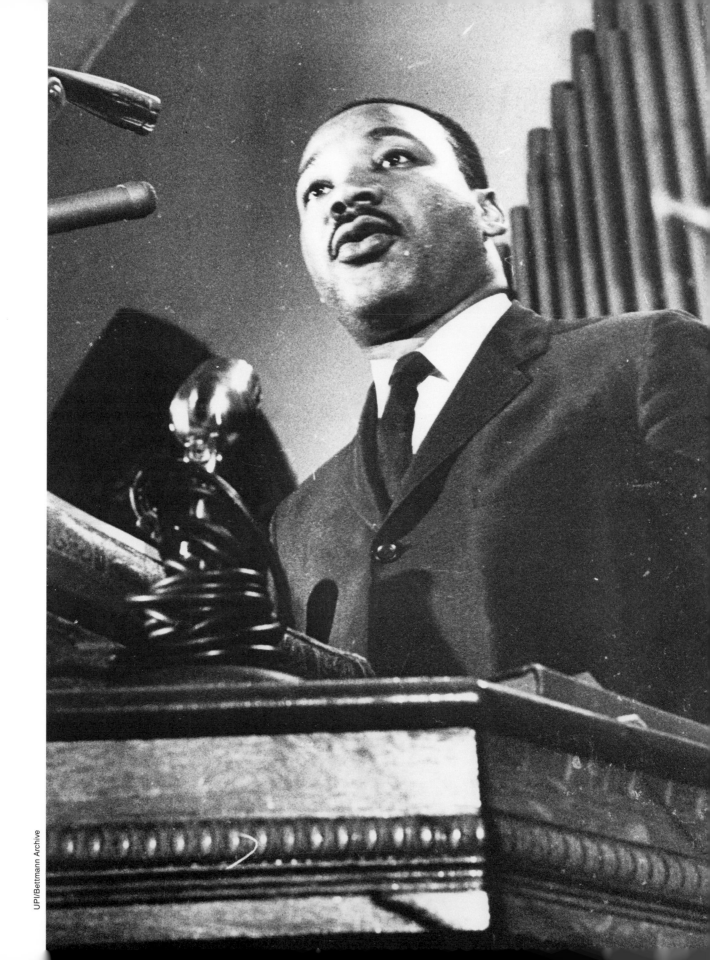

against black demonstrators. Lingo had said, "We don't believe in making arrests. It's better to break them up." In a few minutes, Lingo and Clark would have a chance to put their beliefs into practice. Governor Wallace had already asked them to "use whatever force was necessary" to stop the march.

On the sidelines stood some fifty white spectators. Beside a yellow bus, some distance from the troopers, about fifty blacks also watched. The marchers kept moving across the bridge. Glancing down into the cold, muddy-yellow waters of the Alabama River, Hosea Williams said to John Lewis, "I hope you can swim, 'cause we're fixing to end up in it."

The marchers kept moving. First they were seventy feet, then sixty feet away from the troopers. When they were fifty feet away, Major John Cloud, in charge of the troopers, ordered the marchers to stop.

He told them to return to their church or to their homes.

Hosea Williams asked to have a word with him.

The major replied, "There is no word to be had."

Twice more the two men repeated this exchange. Finally, the major said that the marchers had two minutes to turn around.

No one moved. Several seconds passed, and then the major's voice broke the silence. "Troopers, advance," he said.

What happened next was to affect Americans all over the country. It was also to affect the president and the Congress, leading to the Voting Rights Act of 1965. What happened next led observers to refer to March 7, 1965, as "Bloody Sunday."

Before finding out what did happen on the Edmund Pettus Bridge that afternoon, let us trace the road that brought the marchers there.

The Reverend Dr. Martin Luther King, Jr.

1

THE ROAD TO SELMA

Before 1960 Joseph Atlas made his living farming in East Carroll Parish, Louisiana. After 1960 Joseph Atlas had trouble making a living from farming. That year Atlas had testified before the U.S. Civil Rights Commission as to why no blacks were registered to vote in East Carroll. Shortly thereafter, local merchants refused to gin Joseph Atlas's cotton. They also refused to sell him supplies. The merchants were white. Atlas was black.

Ernestine Talbert, a black woman, taught school in Greene County, Mississippi. One day she attempted to register to

Looking over the Mississippi voter-registration form, 1964

vote in nearby George County. Shortly afterward, the all-white local school board fired her.

Joseph Atlas and Ernestine Talbert both lived in the part of the South called the Black Belt, an area stretching from southern Virginia to northern Louisiana and southeastern Arkansas.

The Black Belt, originally named for its rich, dark soil, was also the area where the highest percentage of black Southerners lived. It was where black voter registration was the lowest. In 1960 these numbers ranged from 5 percent of voting-age blacks in Mississippi to 37 percent in Arkansas.

Why was black registration so low? After all, blacks did have a constitutional right to vote.

Yet most blacks in the South remained unregistered. This was especially true in the states of the Deep South: Alabama, Louisiana, Mississippi, and South Carolina. Here, blacks feared reprisals from the whites who controlled voter registration. Sometimes, opponents of the black vote used economic pressures to prevent blacks from voting. Since most Southern blacks depended economically on whites, the threatened loss of income was often enough to stop them from registering. Joseph Atlas and Ernestine Talbert were the victims of such pressure.

If such measures didn't work, there was always the threat of physical force. Throughout the South, blacks who tried to register often received anonymous death threats. Sometimes these threats were realized. In 1957, bombings and burnings persuaded nine out of ten registered blacks in one Florida county to remove their names from the rolls.

Still, the most effective ways to stop blacks from voting were actually legal. Before 1965 only local registrars could enroll new voters. In the South these officials had almost complete power to determine whether a person had the necessary qualifications to vote.

What were these qualifications? They varied from state to state, from county to county, but the reality was that in the South blacks had a much harder time qualifying than whites.

To keep blacks from registering, some states added a literacy requirement. A potential voter had to satisfy the registrar that he or she could read, write, and understand what was written. In Mississippi a potential voter was required to interpret any section of the state's constitution that the registrar required. If the registrar felt that the person was unable either to read or to understand it, the person would not be registered. Mississippi registrars regularly asked blacks to interpret difficult sections of the constitution. Whites were given the easier questions. Even if a black seemed to understand the section, the registrar nearly always declared that he or she didn't comprehend it. If a white had trouble, the registrar regularly permitted him or her to vote anyway.

The literacy requirements worked very effectively and kept most blacks from even attempting to register. But what about those black people who had managed somehow to register? Could something be done to remove them from the rolls? The answer was yes. Throughout the 1950s, Louisiana registrars examined applications that had been approved. They were looking for errors and omissions. If they found them, they could take away someone's right to vote. Moreover, the only person who judged whether these errors existed was the registrar. If a registrar said there were errors, then there were errors. Thus, some blacks who had been voters suddenly found that they had lost that right.

By the late 1950s, the situation was so severe that the federal government stepped in and tried to reduce or eliminate barriers to black voting. The Civil Rights Act of 1957 marked the government's first attempt. Among other provisions, the act established a nonpartisan Civil Rights Commission and added a civil-rights division to the Justice Department, giving the attorney general of the United States the power to prosecute violators of voting rights in the federal district courts.

The new act's weaknesses quickly became clear. It took the Justice Department a long time to try individual cases. First the department had to receive a complaint; then it had to investigate the complaint

Mrs. Rosa Parks, whose refusal to move to the back of a bus on December 1, 1955, led to the year-long Montgomery bus boycott

Dr. King at police headquarters in Albany, Georgia, 1962, after his arrest

and gather evidence. Usually, a registrar's records made up a large part of the evidence, and most Southern registrars delayed the turning over of requested records. In addition, the Eisenhower administration was reluctant to pursue civil-rights cases, and between 1957 and 1960 only four cases of voting-rights violations reached the federal courts. By the end of the latter year, throughout the South, the federal government had failed to assist even one person in voting.

In 1960 another Civil Rights Act was passed. Now the right of the federal government to examine voting registers was stated more clearly. In this way the government hoped to shorten some of the delays in turning records over. Formerly, a regis-

trar could claim that the records were missing. The new act made it harder for such deception to occur.

Another part of the act permitted the Justice Department to seek a "pattern or practice" decision from the courts. Under this provision, the federal government did not have to rely on one case to prove all its points. Federal prosecutors could claim, for example, that sixteen people in a county lost their jobs after they tried to register, thus demonstrating an overall pattern or practice of discrimination, which is generally easier than proving its existence in one case.

Finally, the Civil Rights Act of 1960 said, among other things, that states could be sued for voting-rights violations. Before, only individuals could be sued. Federal officials felt that this part of the act would allow them to deal with the larger source of discrimination against blacks: state and local anti-civil-rights measures and those who wrote and enforced them.

Unfortunately, the Civil Rights Act of 1960 failed to bring about the desired results. Opponents—whether as advocates of states' rights or of white supremacy, or of both—once again found ways of getting around the legislation. Registrars still refused to give up their records. Also, the "pattern or practice" provision didn't help as much as expected in the prosecution of cases.

Civil-rights groups began to get restless. The process of bringing cases before the courts moved very slowly, and the federal government's attempts to persuade Southern officials before suing them slowed matters even more.

The federal government hoped that civil-rights groups would be able to advance voter registration at the state and local levels. By the early 1960s, in fact, a number of voter-registration drives were already under way. The Southern Regional Council, for example, organized the Voters Education Project. Their efforts resulted in a considerable increase in black voter registration between 1962 and 1964.

In 1964 came the greatest effort so far. It was the year of the Mississippi Freedom Summer. Workers went from door to door canvassing blacks. Intense fear and very limited success characterized the summer. The threat of violence was in the air. Just before Freedom Summer began, three civil-rights workers—two of them white, one black—had been murdered. By its end, thirty-five shootings had been reported, along with three more murders and scores of beatings. Homes and other buildings had been bombed; churches had been burned. More than ever the country became aware of the plight of blacks seeking the right to vote.

Freedom Summer did have another important result. As the summer wore on, the anger of civil-rights leaders increased. The target of their anger was the federal government. They had been promised protection. Where was it? Federal officials defended themselves by saying they could not intrude in state affairs.

By 1964 it was clear that the tactic of using the courts simply wasn't working. Though prosecutors had been able to avoid dealing with prejudiced local

"A badge of servitude"

In 1891, a man named Homer Plessy boarded a train in Louisiana and took a seat in a passenger coach. Plessy was part Negro, the coach was for "Whites Only," and he was asked to move to a coach reserved for blacks. He refused, was arrested, and his case went to court.

Some sixty years later, in Topeka, Kansas, a black girl named Linda Brown went to enroll in her local elementary school. She was refused admission. She and her parents sued the local school board, and her case, too, went to court.

Both Mr. Plessy and Miss Brown lost their cases in the local courts, but each used the *right of appeal* to higher courts, and eventually their cases were heard by the United States Supreme Court. The decisions of the Supreme Court in *Plessy versus Ferguson* (1896) and *Brown versus Board of Education of Topeka* (1954) are two of the most important in the history of the Court and of our nation.

The issue in both cases was *segregation*. From the end of slavery in 1863 on into the present century, it was common practice throughout the country, and especially in the South, to maintain separate facilities for blacks and whites in most areas of daily life, from schools to hotels to water fountains. This *customary* practice of discrimination, known as *de facto discrimination*, was often written into state laws that made separation of the races *mandatory* in schools, restaurants, and other public facilities. This is known as *de jure discrimination—de jure* is Latin for "by right" or "by law"—and it was the *constitutionality* of these state laws that the Supreme Court was deciding on in 1896 and again in 1954.

In the Plessy case, the Court voted 8 to 1 to uphold the Louisiana law requiring separate facilities for blacks on railroad trains. The *majority decision* of the eight justices stated that maintaining *separate but equal* facilities for blacks did not violate the Fourteenth Amendment to the Constitution, which guarantees *equal protection of the laws* to all citizens.

The one justice who thought the Louisiana law was *unconstitutional* was John Marshall Harlan, himself a former slave owner from Kentucky. In his *dissenting opinion*, Harlan stated that to force a member of one race to use separate facilities was in effect to place on that person a "badge of servitude." Thus, Harlan reasoned, separate is *not* equal.

In the Brown case, the justices unanimously overruled the Plessy case and the "separate but equal" doctrine. They ordered segregated schools to be integrated "with all deliberate speed," and the case served as the basis for overruling many state segregation laws.

But even with the power of a court order, progress in *integration* was slow. By 1964, ten years after the Brown decision, only twenty-one black children were in mixed schools in Alabama; there was not one mixed school in all of Mississippi; and throughout the eleven states of the South, only one black child in one hundred went to school with whites.

For this reason, black leaders in the 1950s and 1960s realized that their efforts to bring pressure on the federal government to enforce *desegregation* would not be enough; they would have to use *direct action*, in the form of sit-ins, boycotts, and demonstrations, to bring about integration and full equality of black citizens before the law.

Spectators (left) observing an orderly civil-rights march in Albany, Georgia, 1962

judges, many of the federal district court judges in the South proved every bit as prejudiced as their local counterparts. The Justice Department often found itself pleading its case before a judge who took months to read the evidence, then requested more evidence, then took more months to read the new evidence, and so on. These purposeful delays continued to frustrate the Justice Department in its efforts to increase black voter registration.

In the past decade, new strategies for change had evolved throughout the South as blacks pushed for an end to segregation. In 1955–56, in Montgomery, Alabama, blacks had boycotted city buses to protest segregated seating on them. (By law, blacks had to sit in the rear of public buses.) Led by a twenty-seven-year-old minister named Martin Luther King, Jr., Montgomery's blacks used the nonviolent tactics of demonstration, passive resistance, and "direct action" to bring attention to their cause. During the successful 382-day boycott, they discovered that the mass arrests that resulted from demonstrations helped to unify the black community and to gain the sympathy of many whites across the nation.

The lessons of Montgomery were not lost on young, black Southerners frustrated by old methods. In 1960, black col-

Demonstrators duck away from the spray of fire hoses in Birmingham, May 3, 1963.

lege students staged the first "sit-in" at a segregated lunch counter in Greensboro, North Carolina. Soon, sit-ins were occurring all over the South—at lunch counters, department stores, theaters, supermarkets, libraries. All over, the protesters used the same tactics, which involved sitting in at facilities restricted to whites and refusing to move or to fight back when attacked—tactics they learned from Dr. King.

Two years later, Dr. King and others from the Southern Christian Leadership Conference joined a series of demonstrations under way in Albany, Georgia. Their purpose was not only to end segregation but to force the hiring of blacks for city jobs and the creation of a biracial commission on desegregation.

By the end of 1962, more than two thousand blacks had gone to jail for their part in the Albany protests. The protesters had used the tactics of the boycott and the sit-in, and with the arrival of Dr. King in Albany, a new tactic was employed—that of the mass demonstration. But the Albany campaign was not counted as successful. City officials managed to avoid bad publicity by confining police violence to the outlying barns and pastures that served as detention centers; at the demonstrations themselves, arrests were carried out relatively quietly. The federal government refused to intervene in Albany, and although the campaign had some small successes in closing down segregated facilities, the goal of establishing lasting integration in Albany had not been achieved.

Dr. King and others from the Albany campaign moved on to Birmingham, Alabama, in the spring of 1963. The goals were to be those they had sought in Albany, in addition to amnesty for the demonstrators. This time, a more careful plan of action was worked out by the movement's leaders than had been the case in Albany. This time, too, they faced a different kind of law-enforcement officer.

Before the Birmingham demonstrations had run their course, the city's commissioner of public safety, Eugene T. "Bull" Connor, had used cattle prods, fire hoses, sticks, and police dogs against the demonstrators. In doing so, he caused such havoc in Birmingham—and brought such outside attention—that city authorities agreed, on May 10, 1963, to meet some of the blacks' demands in exchange for a halt to the demonstrations. But the truce did not last. In the months that followed, white racists retaliated through continued bombings and beatings, and on a Sunday morning in September, four young black girls were killed and many people injured when a bomb went off in a Birmingham church.

In Birmingham, civil-rights leaders learned that they would have to confront the most notoriously racist white officials in the most deeply racist of communities if they were to gain widespread attention and sympathy for their cause. The movement so far had brought attention to conditions of segregation, poverty, and unemployment, and in late 1964 Dr. King and other leaders decided to turn their attention to the issue of voting rights. The jurisdiction they chose was one of the region's most thoroughly segregated: Dallas County, Alabama, whose sheriff was James G. Clark and whose county seat was Selma.

"A firm league of friendship"

John C. Calhoun

Opponents of civil rights for blacks during the 1950s and '60s, in the Deep South and elsewhere, had a time-honored political idea around which to rally. This was the doctrine of *states' rights*.

The story of states' rights is one of resistance to central authority. Throughout U.S. history, advocates of this idea have argued that the nation is actually a *voluntary compact* of states, that each state has the right to make and enforce its own laws, and that the powers of the federal government should be strictly limited in local matters.

Before the founding of the republic, during the war for independence, several of the thirteen colonies ignored the commands of the Continental Congress, claiming that their militias were independent and would fight the war as each colony saw fit to do. Once independence was won, and it came time to work out the form the new republic would take, what the founding fathers arrived at was not a constitution but rather the *Articles of Confederation*, which allowed for a "firm league of friendship" among the thirteen former colonies.

By 1787 the founding fathers realized that the powers of the national government had to be made more specific, and they called the Federal Convention for this purpose. The Constitution of the United States was the result. The federal government came out of the convention with broader powers, but states' rights were still provided for, mostly in the form of the Tenth Amendment to the Constitution—the final amendment in the Bill of Rights—which states that "powers not delegated to the United States by the Constitution...are reserved to the States, respectively, or to the people."

In the years that followed, many conflicts arose over the issue of federal versus states' rights. A severe challenge to national authority arose in 1828, when a federal tariff, or tax, was passed that the Southern states saw as a penalty to them in favor of Northern industry. In 1832, South Carolina, led by former vice-president John C. Calhoun, passed an ordinance of *nullification*, which stated that federal attempts to collect the tax would be resisted by the state militia. President Andrew Jackson made it clear that federal forces would be sent to South Carolina to enforce the law, and in 1833 a *compromise* was reached. The compromise allowed for a reduction in the tariff itself but maintained the federal government's right to tax the states.

Armed conflict was avoided in the nullification controversy, but the question of state versus federal authority persisted. In the 1840s and '50s, the anti-slavery movement was growing. The slaveholding states of the South responded to the *abolitionists* by claiming that the legality of slavery was for the individual states to determine, and not a federal matter. The assertion of these states' rights over this and other issues eventually went beyond nullification to the *secession* of the eleven Southern states in 1860–61 and the outbreak of civil war.

From the 1860s on, the increasing size of the country and periodic involvement in foreign wars further strengthened federal authority. But the states'-rights position has continued to be put forth throughout this century, and nowhere was it put forth with more vigor and determination than in Selma, Alabama, in 1965, through the voices of Governor George Wallace and of thousands of his constituents.

George C. Wallace

2

COME BY SELMA, LORD

In 1965 the governor of Alabama was a small, dark-haired man named George Corley Wallace. Wallace strongly backed the policies of segregation. In turn, Selma's new mayor, Joseph Smitherman, loyally backed his governor. In Selma, though, people viewed the thirty-five-year-old Smitherman as a moderate. This did not mean that the mayor disapproved of segregation; it did mean that he believed that a soft approach would best preserve it. Direct confrontation between blacks and whites would damage segregation. It would make white Southerners seem bru-

Inside Brown's Chapel Methodist Church, Selma, 1965

tal and would arouse sympathy for blacks.

Smitherman had heard that blacks were targeting his city for a voting drive, and he wanted another moderate to be his commissioner of public safety. He thought he had found the right person in Captain J. Wilson Baker.

A large, even-tempered man, Baker accepted the position. Baker pledged to keep the peace, "some way, somehow." But if Baker wanted a calm Selma, one man would have to be carefully watched.

That man was Jim Clark. The county sheriff was a large man, and renowned for his bad temper. His rough tactics had already caused trouble with blacks. To make matters worse, Clark had his own

25

J. Wilson Baker (left) and Jim Clark

volunteer posse to call on to "preserve law and order."

Now that trouble loomed, Mayor Smitherman tried to get around Sheriff Clark. Formerly, the sheriff had been responsible for all law-enforcement activities in Selma. In the future he would divide this responsibility with Baker. Smitherman ordered Clark to take charge of civil-rights actions only around the courthouse. Baker would handle any other situations. Moreover, Baker would direct the city police. Jim Clark did not like this new arrangement, and in the months to come, friction between Baker and Clark grew rapidly.

On January 2, 1965, Martin Luther King spoke to some seven hundred blacks in Brown's Chapel Methodist Church. In the following three months, Brown's would nourish the deeply religious spirit of the demonstrators. From the pulpit, their leaders, most of them Southern Baptist ministers, would encourage them. In times of joy and anguish, the demonstrators and the whole black community would gather there to sing spirituals, to embrace one another, to draw strength from their faith.

Now, on January 2, Dr. King looked down at the faces lifted up to him and said, "We must be willing to go to jail by the thousands in Alabama."

The drive began on Monday, January 18. Led by King, four hundred marched the few blocks from the church to the Dallas County courthouse, where new voters were registered. Clark, Smitherman, and Baker were waiting for them. Some of the marchers kept their eyes on the clubs carried by nearby officers.

Baker spoke first. He informed King that Selma did not permit parades. The marchers then broke into small groups and walked away. The first confrontation was over in minutes. To the mayor's relief, it had ended peacefully.

The rest of the day was not quite so calm. After the marchers had dispersed, King went to check in at the Albert Hotel—the first black person ever to do so. In the lobby, a white man struck him. Quickly, Wilson Baker dragged the man away.

Despite this incident, January 18 had passed without widespread violence. Clark had looked like a "caged tiger," but he had kept his temper in check.

Tuesday proved to be different. The previous day, Clark had led demonstrators to an alley beside the courthouse and instructed them to wait there to be registered.

Normally, applicants waited in corridors or along the street. Tuesday's demonstrators refused to return to Clark's alley.

Dr. King speaking from the pulpit of Brown's Chapel. To his immediate left is Coretta Scott King, his wife.

Local police and demonstrators outside the Dallas County courthouse

Angrily, the sheriff grabbed one woman, Amelia Boynton, by the neck and pushed her along for half a block before putting her inside a patrol car. The next day both the New York *Times* and the Washington *Post* carried photos of the incident.

The other demonstrators began to move about excitedly. Deputies with nightsticks and electric cattle prods moved toward them. In the skirmish that followed, the officers arrested sixty-seven marchers for unlawful assembly and criminal provocation.

Dr. King had watched the events from a car across the street. After the arrests, he entered the courthouse and asked, in vain, for an injunction against the sheriff, saying that the arrests were unlawful. By now it was clear that Sheriff Clark was growing impatient with Captain Baker's strategy of delaying but not provoking those blacks who sought to register.

For Wednesday's protest, the organizers decided to have the marchers descend

County sheriff Clark on the courthouse steps

on the courthouse in three separate groups. Clark ordered that they line up at an entrance no one else used, and the marchers refused. The sheriff's temper smoldered. He warned the marchers that they would be arrested if they did not disperse in one minute and then began to count the seconds off out loud. At "sixty," he arrested the first group of marchers.

The second group met the same fate, and when the third began to move across the street, Clark called to Baker, "Will you clear them away? They are blocking the sidewalk."

By this time, Baker and Clark were glaring at each other. Baker saw Clark getting himself into deeper and deeper trouble. Clark felt Baker was too soft. Neither thought the other should be in charge. Yet somehow they had to work together. Otherwise, the protesters might prevail.

Baker then tried a compromise. He said that the marchers could gather at the front entrance, but only if they didn't block the sidewalk. They agreed, but Sheriff Clark didn't, and he had them arrested.

On Friday, January 22, 105 black teachers marched to the courthouse. Clark and his deputies used their nightsticks to push the first line of demonstrators off the court-house steps. An NBC cameraman recorded the action for the entire country to see. The teachers had achieved their goal. They had risked their jobs to march against voter discrimination. Some attention had been brought to Selma, Alabama. At the end of the first week of demonstrations, there had been more than two hundred arrests, and still not a single black had been added to the voting register.

On Monday of the next week, in front of the courthouse, Annie Lee Cooper, a fifty-three-year-old black woman, stepped from the line of protesters and knocked Clark down with a punch to the head. Three deputies grabbed Mrs. Cooper and wrestled her to the ground. "I wish you would hit me, you scum," Mrs. Cooper shouted. Clark whacked her on the head with his club. One reporter wrote that the sound was so loud that it "was heard through the crowd gathered on the street." Now it was clear that the demonstrators were growing impatient along with their nemesis, Jim Clark.

That night, SCLC leaders decided it was the right time for Dr. King to get him-

Clark (hatless) and deputies subdue Annie Lee Cooper on the courthouse lawn.

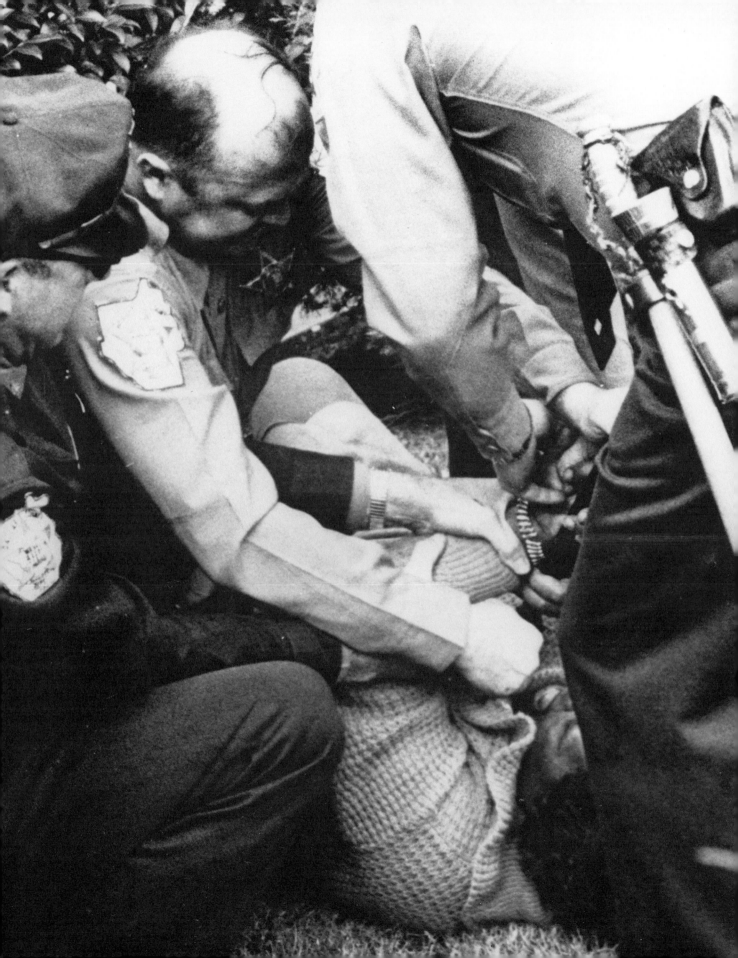

self arrested. It was simply another way to increase the pressure on Clark and the city government. On February 1, King and 250 followers marched downtown. Instead of walking in a long line, two abreast, the group marched as one. They knew that they were breaking the city's regulation against parades. Wilson Baker arrested King along with some seven hundred others.

On Wednesday, February 3, several hundred teenagers boycotted high school for the third straight day. Scores of others had been jailed during Monday and Tuesday's demonstrations, and Charles Mauldin, a seventeen-year-old from Hudson High School, led three hundred students to the courthouse. When they saw the sheriff, they sang, "Ain't gonna let Jim Clark turn me round," followed by other protest songs.

The sheriff listened for about thirty minutes. Then he bellowed through his loudspeaker the familiar words "You are under arrest."

From the beginning, children and teenagers had played an important role in the voting-rights drives. Boys and girls as young as eight years old had marched, and some had even participated before their parents did. During the first three months of 1965, the children learned their most important lessons outside of school. They learned about courage in Brown's Chapel and in the streets leading to the courthouse. They learned about it from their teachers, who also marched, and from the movement's leaders they learned about perseverance and discipline. On February 2 and 3, they learned what it felt like to be arrested, to be incarcerated in the downtown armory, to be taken to appear before a judge.

Naturally, this put a lot of pressure on the children, and some civil-rights workers were opposed to their participation in demonstrations. One night, eight-year-old Sheyann Webb wrote a note expressing her fears:

> Sheyann Webb, 8 years, was killed today in Selma. She was one of Dr. King Freedom Fighters. She was a student at Clark School, Selma. Sheyann want all people to be free and happy.

Sheyann's mother read the note and made sure that her daughter always marched within her sight.

From jail, Martin Luther King wrote a full-page letter that appeared in the New York *Times*. In it, he appealed for support. He wrote:

> This is Selma, Alabama. There are more Negroes in jail with me than there are on the voting rolls.

King's letter prompted President Lyndon Johnson to hold a news conference, during which he declared, "All of us should be concerned with the efforts of our fellow Americans to register to vote in Alabama."

On February 5, King left jail. The cycle of mass arrests continued, however. Five days later, Clark arrested 165 more teenagers. This time he changed their route to jail. He sent them on a forced march several miles out into the country. Along the way, his deputies used nightsticks and cattle prods to push them along. The deputies wouldn't let any of the teenagers stop to rest. Only after several miles of this punishment did they release the exhausted youths.

The weeks of demonstrations and arrests had made Selma edgy. Jim Clark was edgy, too. On February 2, he entered the hospital with chest pains. The doctors diagnosed the problem as indigestion.

Civil-rights leaders discuss strategy in a Selma hotel room. In shirtsleeves is James Forman, of SNCC; to his left are the Reverend Ralph D. Abernathy, of SCLC, and Dr. King.

Children and teenagers marching in Selma

Black children prayed for him at the court-house, beneath signs that read "Freedom Now." When Clark left the hospital, he wore a badge with one word on it. The word was "Never."

The violence spread to nearby Marion, Alabama. On February 18, black demonstrators had a bloody confrontation with state troopers, during which a trooper shot twenty-six-year-old Jimmie Lee Jackson in the stomach. Seven days later, Jackson died in a Selma hospital.

Three thousand mourners attended two services held for Jackson in Selma and Marion. A chill rain fell, for this part of Alabama was in its stormy season.

The next march scheduled was from Selma to the state capital, Montgomery, to protest to Governor Wallace the lack of black voter registration. The date set for it was March 7. On Saturday, the day before the march, jonquils and forsythias began to bloom along the roadside. Spring was near, but on the far side of a bitter storm.

The n-double-a-c-p, core, and snick

Civil-rights organizations large and small, from different parts of the country, were represented at demonstrations at Selma and elsewhere throughout the South. Students for a Democratic Society (SDS), a predominantly white organization of college students, sent delegations from the North and the Midwest. Marching alongside the students were ministers and rabbis, lawyers from the National Urban League, and entertainers from the makeshift Folksingers' Caravan.

Along with the Southern Christian Leadership Conference (SCLC), organized by Dr. King in 1957, perhaps the most prominent groups at Selma in 1965 were the NAACP, CORE, and SNCC.

The National Association for the Advancement of Colored People (NAACP) was formed in 1909 as a direct result of the lynching of a black man in Illinois. Membership was black and white, though in its early years the association was headed by seven white men and one black man, W. E. B. Du Bois. The association was known best for its work through legal channels, and NAACP lawyers were influential in winning favorable decisions in school-desegregation cases and in getting the federal government to act in the Montgomery bus boycott in 1956. For the most part, the NAACP did not employ tactics of direct action and demonstration. But in 1960, when four members of the association's Youth Councils staged a sit-in at a lunch counter in Greensboro, North Carolina, the association backed the students and encouraged participation in the growing protest movement.

During the 1940s, James Farmer was race-relations secretary of the Fellowship of Reconciliation (FOR), a pacifist organization founded during the First World War. In 1943 Farmer and other members of FOR formed the Congress of Racial Equality (CORE), which was dedicated to working for civil rights for blacks through the methods of nonviolence. In 1947, CORE members organized a protest against segregation on buses in North Carolina. Known as the "Journey of Reconciliation," this action was the forerunner of the Freedom Rides sponsored by CORE during the early 1960s. Membership in CORE had always been biracial, but after 1965 the organization began to favor the principles of *black nationalism,* and to reflect this change, leadership of the organization was restricted to blacks.

In 1960, at the urging of Dr. King and the SCLC, 200 delegates from 52 colleges and 37 high schools met at Raleigh, North Carolina, and formed the Student Nonviolent Coordinating Committee (SNCC). Although membership in SNCC was biracial, most of its members were Southern blacks. During the early 1960s, SNCC was responsible for organizing sit-ins and demonstrations in more than a hundred communities. In places like Birmingham and Selma, the actions of SNCC members set the stage for the mass demonstrations that took place on the arrival of Dr. King and other prominent leaders. Like CORE, SNCC and its leadership began to regard the tactics of nonviolence as overly cautious and slow, and in the years after the Selma campaign, prominent members of SNCC such as Stokely Carmichael, James Forman, and H. Rap Brown went on to promote the more militant principles of *Afro-Americanism* and *black power.*

3

THE VIEW FROM THE BRIDGE

"Troopers, advance." Major Cloud's voice broke the silence. Immediately, the troopers obeyed the order and rushed forward. One observer wrote that on March 7, the troopers "moved with such force they seemed almost to pass over the waiting column instead of through it."

John Lewis, hit in the head with a club, was one of the first marchers to fall near Edmund Pettus Bridge. Others among the first ten or twenty blacks at the bridge were swept to the ground. Everywhere people

Troopers and possemen on the far causeway of Edmund Pettus Bridge, March 7, 1965

were screaming and crying. Backpacks and bags were scattered about the pavement.

Those still standing moved backward. The troopers continued to push the marchers, prodding them with nightsticks. A cheer went up from the whites watching from the sidelines.

Then the mounted possemen dug their spurs into their horses. They galloped into the mass of retreating marchers. One girl later recalled that she was terrified the horses would trample her. Marchers huddled together for protection. The sound of their crying mixed

37

John Lewis, of SNCC, being beaten during the retreat from Edmund Pettus Bridge

with the cheers from the white onlookers.

Then a new sound was heard. It echoed like a gunshot. A gray cloud coated both the troopers and the marchers. Someone yelled, "Tear gas." The cloud spread until it covered the highway like a thick fog.

Newsmen a hundred yards away had trouble seeing through it. They were just able to make out about fifty nightsticks raining down on the marchers' heads, shoulders, backs. Coughing and sobbing, the demonstrators broke and ran. They stumbled away from the battlefield as a defeated, unarmed army.

Troopers and possemen pursued them. More tear-gas bombs were released. It became impossible to see. Within minutes, the possemen and troopers had rounded up most of the marchers retreating toward Brown's Chapel in Selma. Four or five women still lay on the grass strip where the troopers had knocked them down. One of these women was Amelia Boynton, who weeks earlier had been dragged from the courthouse steps to a patrol car. Two troopers ordered the women to get up. The women didn't respond, and the troopers set off another tear-gas bomb. The women rose. Blindly, they stumbled across the road.

Meanwhile, the marchers continued to retreat into Selma. Finally, the fleeing blacks reached Sylvan Street, in the black district. The possemen tried to get them off the street and into Brown's Chapel, a block away, clubbing them as they did so. Others from the posse began to beat a cadence on the hoods of nearby cars, shouting, "Get out of town."

A number of blacks could not take it anymore. They hurled bricks and bottles

Tear gas engulfs a roadway in Selma on Bloody Sunday.

A gas-masked trooper orders felled marchers to continue the retreat to Brown's Chapel.

at their tormentors. Wilson Baker intervened. He persuaded the marchers to enter the church and urged Sheriff Clark to stop the assaults.

The scene inside the church was one of turmoil. The parsonage next door had been transformed into an emergency ward. Marchers lay on the floor, crying and moaning. Doctors and nurses administered first aid. They washed burning eyes with boric-acid solution. There were

arm and leg fractures, and many cuts and bruises. Among others, John Lewis had been felled with a possible skull fracture. Mrs. Boynton lay semiconscious on a table.

Outside, hundreds of blacks gathered. They had rushed to the church as news of the incident spread. The mood of the crowd was tense and angry. Black leaders

Amelia Boynton being helped to her feet after the attack at the bridge

"Because injustice is here"

"Nonviolence is the answer to the crucial political and moral question of our time—the need for man to overcome oppression and violence without resorting to violence and oppression."

Mohandas K. Gandhi

These were the words of the Reverend Dr. Martin Luther King, Jr., upon his acceptance of the Nobel Peace Prize. The speech was delivered in Oslo, Norway, December 10, 1964, just three weeks before King traveled to Selma to join in civil-rights protests there.

To Dr. King, nonviolence and passive resistance were more than just tactics; they were ideas that had been argued and tested throughout history. In his writings and speeches, King referred often to the nonviolent approach of Jesus and his disciples, to their *passive resistance* to Roman authorities, and to the *redemption* protesters achieved when they suffered at the hands of the authorities.

The figure from history who most directly influenced Dr. King was Mohandas K. Gandhi, the leader of the independence movement in India who was assassinated in 1948, the year King graduated from college. The Mahatma (a title of respect in India) had used the tactic of *civil disobedience* to protest racist conditions in South Africa as long ago as 1907. In India, in 1930, he led hundreds of thousands of his countrymen on a 200-mile march, to protest Britain's control over India's natural resources. This and later actions led by Gandhi resulted in India's independence from British rule in 1947.

Of Dr. King's writings, one of the most famous and influential is his "Letter from Birmingham City Jail," written April 16, 1963. King addressed the letter to his "dear fellow clergymen," many of whom objected to the tactic of *direct action* in confronting the authorities, however unjust their laws. This letter remains one of history's clearest statements of the doctrine of nonviolence. It states, in part:

"I am in Birmingham because injustice is here. . . . Just as the Apostle Paul left his village of Tarsus and carried the gospel of Jesus Christ to the far corners of the Greco-Roman world, so am I compelled to carry the gospel of freedom beyond my own home town."

"In our own nation, the Boston Tea Party represented a massive act of civil disobedience."

"One has not only a legal but a moral responsibility to obey just laws. Conversely, one has a moral responsibility to disobey unjust laws. . . . One who breaks an unjust law must do so openly, lovingly, and with a willingness to accept the penalty."

moved among the people. They asked them to stay calm and to remember the nonviolent purpose of the drive.

The sight of more than a hundred possemen at the end of the block hardly calmed the crowd. Tensions rose as the troops seemed to be grouping into an attack formation. However, they left after an hour.

As night descended, the area was once again populated entirely by blacks. From the housing project and smaller homes nearby came more than nine hundred people. Many held on to each other, weeping. Some appeared in a state of shock.

Hosea Williams spoke; then John Lewis. "I don't know how President Johnson can send troops to Vietnam," Lewis said, "and can't send troops to Selma." Lewis then left for the hospital.

Hosea Williams announced there would be another march to Montgomery on Tuesday. The final words belonged to Martin Luther King. Arriving before Tuesday, he prepared his people for what lay ahead:

We've gone too far to turn back now. We must let them know that nothing can stop us—not even death itself. We must be ready for a season of suffering.

4

THE BRIDGE TO SOMEWHERE

On Monday evening, March 8, George Leonard and his wife sat watching the six-o'clock news. Images of Bloody Sunday crossed the screen. Afterward, Leonard described what he saw:

> The bleeding, broken, and unconscious passed across the screen, some of them limping alone, others supported on either side, still others carried in arms or on stretchers. It was at this point that my wife,

On the road to Montgomery

sobbing, turned and walked away, saying, "I can't look anymore."

Six hours later, George Leonard took the midnight plane from San Francisco to Alabama. At about the same time, hundreds of other Americans were Alabama bound as well. Some of these travelers were white; others were black. All of them had dropped whatever they were doing. Nothing seemed more important than to march alongside the blacks they had seen on their television screens.

In Selma itself, white citizens also reacted strongly to Sunday's events. Some blamed what happened on "outside agitators." Others admitted they were confused. Wasn't Selma like any other place? Even Northern cities like New York had racial problems. Still others didn't want to see or hear any more about it.

Here and there some sympathy for the blacks surfaced. A man reading the paper in a Selma café said, "There's going to be trouble here." He was concerned that the number of injured blacks might rise if there were more confrontations.

Finally, everybody worried about the effect on business. People said that it had already dropped about 25 percent.

Among those officials who were involved, the reaction was also mixed. Governor Wallace declared that by stopping the march he had "saved people's lives." Mayor Smitherman said that he was "in complete accord" with the governor. Wilson Baker, however, dissented. In fact, the day before the Sunday march, he had refused to obey Mayor Smitherman's order to have the city police join the state troopers in using force against the demonstrators. He stated that he would resign rather than carry out such orders. Some members of the city council had then

worked out a compromise. The police would not participate in any violence or use force against the demonstrators, but they would also not intervene in behalf of the demonstrators if the state troopers used force. Jim Clark had always hated the tactics of compromise. He even felt that mass arrests didn't go far enough in curbing the demonstrators. On Sunday, he had finally got his way.

In Washington, too, people stirred. On Monday, six members of Congress condemned the attack on the bridge. The reaction in the nation's capital was important to the black cause. From the start, black leaders needed to use Selma to pressure the federal government. They wanted the president to back an effective new voting-rights bill. When Johnson had become president, he had worked on such a bill. He did not want to rush it through Congress, because he knew he would face Southern opposition. But Bloody Sunday contained a message for the president. Selma was like a time bomb. If he did not act soon, it would explode.

Throughout Monday, Johnson was on the phone about Selma. He was concerned about possible violence during Tuesday's march, and he urged movement leaders to postpone the action. Dr. King's aides were also worried. They feared King might be killed if violence erupted.

No one really knew if the march would take place. Blacks had asked federal judge Frank M. Johnson to lift the ban on a march to Montgomery, and tension continued to mount while everyone waited to hear. Then Judge Johnson contacted the black leaders and recommended that they postpone the march until he could hold hearings, which were to begin on Thursday, to decide if the march should be permitted.

The matter was now left to Dr. King and his associates. Should they postpone?

If they did, they might lose the public's attention. If they went ahead, they would risk King's life and break the law. They decided to postpone.

Sometime Monday, King changed his mind. He announced to the people at Brown's Chapel that he would lead a march on Montgomery the next day. After hours of discussion, at 4:00 A.M. Tuesday, other black leaders agreed to follow his decision. In a little more than ten hours, the second attempt to march on Montgomery would begin.

In the meantime, President Johnson sent LeRoy Collins, director of the Federal Community Relations Service, to Ala-

Dr. King and others stand by as a federal marshal reads the court order prohibiting the Tuesday march to Montgomery.

bama. Collins's task was to try to persuade both sides to compromise. King refused to stop the march. Collins then went to Sheriff Clark and Colonel Lingo. They agreed not to use force against the marchers on one condition—that the marchers turned back when they reached the troopers.

Collins informed King of their promise. King merely smiled in reply.

Time was running out. On Tuesday morning, Judge Johnson banned any march before Thursday. What would King do? At 2:25 P.M., March 9, the answer came. Arriving at Brown's, he stated that he was ready to march. Columns of marchers swiftly formed. At 3:00 P.M., marchers once again reached the Edmund Pettus Bridge.

There, a U.S. marshal read aloud Judge Johnson's order. King said that he would continue the march, and protesters began to move across the bridge. State troopers waited several hundred feet in front of them for the second time that week. Major Cloud stood once again at the head.

The next thing that happened caught

Tuesday, March 9

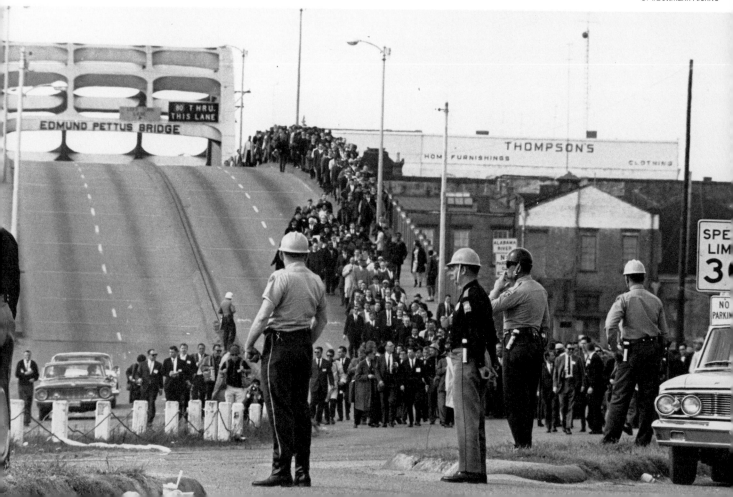

King addresses demonstrators at Brown's Chapel on Tuesday, March 9, after their return from the bridge. At King's right is Andrew Young.

most marchers, newspeople, and onlookers by surprise. King turned back. A moment later, the troopers moved to the side of the highway. The road to Montgomery was open.

It was open, but the marchers were returning, without explanation, to Selma. The columns obediently followed King back. Among many of them, fury mingled with surprise. Had their leader betrayed them? Some realized that the troopers' gesture was one of contempt. Did King have a reason for what he had just done? For the moment, King said nothing.

Washington, meanwhile, was sizzling. Tuesday's newspapers had been filled with angry reactions by Americans to Sunday's attack. Forty-three congressmen and seven senators rose to record their outrage. They urged immediate passage of a new voting-rights act. They also requested the use of federal power to prevent further bloodshed.

Outside the White House, six hundred pickets marched, protesting the federal government's inaction. SNCC members sat in at the Justice Department. Now, within forty-eight hours after Bloody Sun-

49

day, the president issued his first public response to the attack. He said that he was preparing legislation that would secure every American's voting rights. He would complete his recommendations to Congress over the weekend.

Late in the afternoon, events in Selma continued to progress rapidly. Another march to the courthouse was announced for the next day. More than 450 ministers, priests, and rabbis would take part in the demonstration. That evening, violence once again focused the nation's attention on Selma. Several whites attacked four white ministers, including the Reverend James J. Reeb, with clubs. Reeb, from Boston, thirty-eight years old, was rushed to the hospital, unconscious and in critical condition.

On Wednesday, three waves of demonstrators left Brown's for the courthouse. Six nuns from St. Louis led the first group. The demonstrators found Sylvan Street blocked off. Mayor Smitherman and Wilson Baker had decided to ban any marches beyond the Brown's Chapel area.

Five minutes later, two hundred children and teenagers surged forward. The police stopped them, too. A third group met the same fate. The Reverend Ralph D.

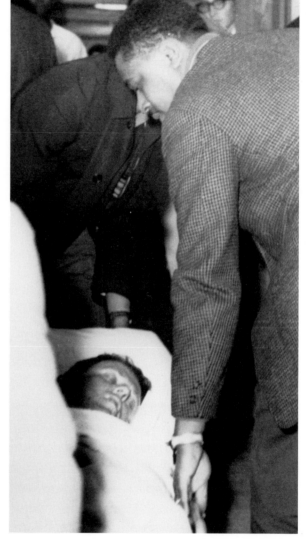

The Reverend James J. Reeb being rushed to the hospital

Abernathy, King's closest associate, announced that the marchers would stay in the street all night.

Sylvan Street that night was an odd sight. About 360 people lay scattered everywhere on inflatable plastic mattresses and under makeshift tents. In the glare of police spotlights they sang the songs that, by this time, the police knew by heart.

In Washington, Thursday, March 11, began quietly. Before the morning ended, twelve civil-rights demonstrators disturbed the calm atmosphere when they began a sit-in on the first floor of the White House. Meanwhile, the president's men and Senate leaders were working out the final details in Johnson's voting-rights proposal.

In Montgomery, on the same day, Judge Johnson began his hearings. King testified that he had halted the march to Montgomery because of a secret agreement. He was referring to the promise Collins had exacted from Lingo and Clark. King certainly had some more explaining to do. The anger of many of the marchers had not died down.

Thursday's late news came from Selma. Reverend Reeb had died at about 9 P.M. Before Reeb died, a worried Wilson Baker had asked James Orange, an assistant to King, "Can you control your people when it happens?" Orange had replied, "The question is, can you control yours."

Yet nobody really knew what the aftermath of Reeb's death would be. As the news spread, blacks poured into Brown's for a memorial service. That night, another cold rain fell on Selma.

On Friday, March 12, the city remained tense. The authorities refused to permit blacks to hold a vigil for Reverend Reeb in front of the courthouse. Sylvan Street remained roped off. Demonstrators could not go beyond it for a second day. They nicknamed the rope the Berlin Wall, and sang:

> The Berlin Wall, the Berlin Wall,
> The wall will come tumbling down.

On the other side of the rope stood scores of sleepy-eyed troopers and city police. An unshaven Wilson Baker was in charge. At 5:00 P.M. he declared that the tents presented a fire hazard and asked that they be taken down. The demonstrators complied.

In Montgomery, Friday marked the second day of Judge Johnson's hearings. Governor Wallace asked to meet with the

Hosea Williams

president, and Johnson replied that he would be willing to see Wallace at any time.

The meeting took place the next day. Wallace blamed the demonstrators for Selma's troubles. He refused to admit that they had any right to protest. President Johnson disagreed. Neither man backed down.

Over the weekend, the president decided to speak before both houses of Congress about his proposed voting-rights bill. He said that he wanted to talk from his "own heart," from his "own experience."

Monday, March 15, turned out to be an historic day in more ways than one. In Alabama, Wilcox and Lowndes Counties registered their first black voters in the twentieth century. (During much of the late nineteenth century, in the aftermath of the Civil War, blacks were able to vote in the South, and a few were even elected to state legislatures and the U.S. House of Representatives.)

In Selma, Wilson Baker arranged for blacks to hold a courthouse rally for Reverend Reeb. Dr. King led the twenty-minute service. It was his first appearance in Selma after his turnabout on the bridge. That evening, Mayor Smitherman had to step between the raised fists of his two chief law enforcers. The bad feelings between Clark and Baker had nearly erupted into a fistfight.

The same evening, about seventy million people watched on television as Lyndon Johnson addressed Congress. The president said, "It is wrong—deadly wrong—to deny any of your fellow Americans the right to vote in this country." Many viewers felt as if the president were speaking directly to them as he continued:

> It is the effort of American Negroes to secure for themselves the full blessing of American life. Their cause must be our cause, too. It is not just Negroes but all of us who must overcome the crippling legacy of bigotry and injustice. And we shall overcome.

He went on to praise black Americans:

> The real hero of the struggle is the American Negro. The cries of pain and the hymns and protests of oppressed people have summoned into convocation all the majesty of this great government.

President Johnson and Governor Wallace (at Johnson's right) meet the press outside the White House following their March 13 meeting on the events at Selma.

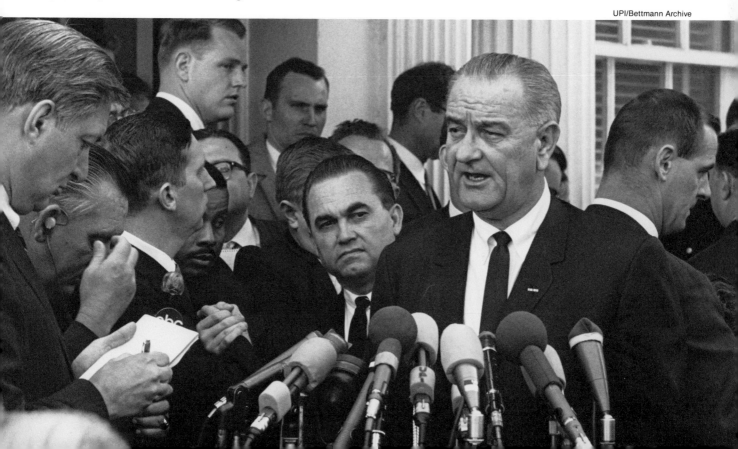

Folksingers Len Chandler (left) and Pete Seeger on the way to Montgomery

The president's words to the nation did not end the troubles, however. The next day, mounted officers assaulted 600 marchers in Montgomery. The attack helped ensure the passage of Johnson's bill. He formally presented it to Congress on Wednesday. Supporters even predicted that half of the South's twenty-two Senators might support it.

That afternoon Judge Johnson also handed down his decision. The demonstrators could march to Montgomery legally on March 21, 1965. At Governor Wallace's request, the president ordered eighteen hundred National Guardsmen to protect them. Bloody Sunday would not be repeated.

Some things about the march seemed familiar. The 3,200 marchers moved down Water Street. Before them stood the Edmund Pettus Bridge, which twice before they had failed to cross. But this time,

Alabama State Capitol, Montgomery, March 21, 1965

54

Federal judge Frank M. Johnson

protected by the National Guard, they crossed it. The road to Montgomery lay open once again.

Three days later, they reached St. Jude, a Roman Catholic conference center outside Montgomery where they were to spend the night. A reporter noted that their entry had an almost biblical grandeur.

The next afternoon, March 25, 1965, Dr. King addressed a crowd of more than 25,000 gathered before the Alabama Statehouse. He said, "This is a shining moment. We are on the move now. We are moving toward the land of freedom."

In the same speech, King warned of a season of suffering still to come. His words

Whites display a Confederate flag in opposition to civil-rights marchers on the road to Montgomery. In the background are members of the National Guard sent to protect the marchers.

Roadside, Montgomery; March 21, 1965

were prophetic. That night, Viola Liuzzo, from Michigan, a mother of five, drove some of the marchers back to Selma. On the return trip to Montgomery, she was shot to death by members of the Ku-Klux Klan.

Still, despite this tragic event, relative quiet reigned the next day in Selma. The events that had begun three months before and climaxed on Bloody Sunday had made voter registration in the South a nationwide concern.

Nearly five months later, on August 6, President Johnson signed the Voting Rights Act of 1965. The act aided not only black voters but also the economically impoverished, the poorly educated, and non-English-speaking minorities. Opposition to the black vote did not end once and for all after Selma and the Voting Rights Act. But now, finally, some two and a half million blacks who had been kept from the ballot box would have the strength of federal law on their side.

We must preserve the right of free assembly but
free assembly does not carry with it

11.

by blocking public thoroughfare

it the right to endanger the safety of others on a public highway.

We do have a right to protest -- and a right to march under conditions that do not infringe the Constitutional rights of our neighbors. I intend to protect all those rights as long as I am permitted to serve in this Office.

We will guard against violence, knowing it strikes from our hands the very weapons with which we seek progress -- obedience to law, and belief in American values.

In Selma as elsewhere we seek peace. We seek order. We seek unity.

But we will not accept the peace of stifled rights, the order imposed by fear, the unity that stifles protest. For peace cannot be purchased at the cost of liberty.

In Selma, as in every city, we are working for just and peaceful settlement. We must remember that after this speech -- after the police and the marshals have gone -- after this bill is passed, the people of Selma must still live and work together. When the attention of the nation has gone elsewhere they must try to heal the wounds and build a new community. This cannot easily be done on a battleground of violence as the history of the South itself shows. It is in recognition of this that men of both races have shown such impressive responsibility in recent days.

AFTERWORD

THE VOTING RIGHTS ACT OF 1965

"At times history and fate meet at a single time in a single place to shape a turning point in man's unending search for freedom. . . . So it was a century ago at Appomattox. So it was last week in Selma, Alabama."

These were the words of President Lyndon Johnson on March 15, 1965, in his speech before Congress just a week after Bloody Sunday. The speech was an urgent call for support of a federal voting-rights

A page from President Johnson's March 15 speech in support of voting-rights legislation. The handwriting is Johnson's.

bill, which took the form of the Voting Rights Act of 1965 and was passed into law on August 6 of that year.

The key to the Voting Rights Act was that it gave the federal government a firmer hand in enforcing voting rights within the states. For one thing, the president himself was empowered to suspend literacy tests in places where they were found to be discriminatory. The act also provided for federal registrars to be sent to the states to enroll black voters.

Most observers agree that the act helped to give blacks access to the vote in the Deep South. In so doing, it changed

Lyndon Johnson delivering the March 15 speech before a joint session of Congress. Behind him is Speaker of the House John McCormack.

forever the politics of that region and of the country as a whole.

Small events often illuminate larger changes. One such small event occurred in 1974, when Sheyann Webb celebrated her eighteenth birthday. Nine years before, Sheyann had marched alongside Martin Luther King, Jr., to protest voting-rights discrimination in Selma. At the time, she had made a promise to herself. Now, having reached voting age, she kept that promise. As soon as she could, Sheyann went to the Dallas County courthouse to register to vote.

No armed possemen stood by ready to use their weapons against her. No sheriff ordered her to stand in the alleyway. Nobody prevented her from registering.

The following year, Sheyann was called into the mayor's office to have her picture taken with Wilson Baker and Joseph Smitherman, who was still Selma's mayor. The photo session was part of a ceremony marking the tenth anniversary of the Selma protest. During the picture-taking, Wilson Baker recalled how Sheyann had "run down and off" the Edmund Pettus Bridge on Bloody Sunday. Then he apologized to the young woman for what had happened that afternoon ten years before.

In June of 1983, another seemingly small event occurred. At the governor's mansion, in Montgomery, the Reverend Jesse Jackson paid a visit to Governor George Wallace, the same Governor Wallace who had tried to prevent the march to Montgomery. This time, however, Wallace did not greet the black leader with state troopers. Instead, he received Jackson warmly, serving his guest pecan rolls on a silver tray and pouring him iced tea from a pitcher.

Surely, as they sat there on the porch of the governor's mansion, both men must have realized how far they had come since the dark days of Selma. They must also have realized that without the voter-registration drive of almost two decades ago, they might not be sitting together at all.

The importance of Selma can be seen most directly in the increase in voter registration since the events of 1965 and passage of the Voting Rights Act. In the ten years after President Johnson signed the act, black voter registration in Selma rose from less than 2 percent of those eligible to 60 percent. Across the South, the number of eligible blacks registered went from 38 percent in 1964 to 62 percent by 1971.

In the twenty years since Selma, black and white politicians alike have become aware of black voter power at both the local and national levels. According to the 1980 Census, some 17 million blacks are of voting age, making up 10.5 percent of the electorate. (Half of these voting-age blacks live in the South.) In 1970, a total of 1,469 blacks held elected office at all levels of government, including 10 in Congress. By 1973, the number had more than tripled,

At the Oval Office in 1966, Dr. King urges President Johnson toward more vigorous enforcement of the Voting Rights Act.

to 5,160, with 21 blacks serving in Congress.

Even more significant, perhaps, in the two decades since Selma, have been the gains in city halls across the nation. In 1983 there were 220 black mayors, 16 of them in cities with populations of more than 100,000. Today black mayors preside in some of the largest and most important of our cities, such as Chicago, Philadelphia, and Los Angeles. There are black mayors in the South as well; for example, Andrew Young, of Atlanta, and Marion Barry, of Washington, D.C.

Still, as black political power has increased, so have the frustrations of many blacks who feel a lingering lack of influence in local and national political life. An important step was taken in 1984, when, for the first time, a black person ran in the presidential primaries of one of the two major political parties. In the North, South, East, and West, Jesse Jackson won votes and, just as important, urged blacks in great numbers to register and vote.

Two decades ago, Martin Luther King, Jr., John Lewis, Hosea Williams, and other black leaders saw the importance of the ballot box to blacks in their quest for equality. So did the thousands of men and women who, along with their children, were stopped twice but not three times on the bridge leading from Selma to Montgomery.

INDEX

Page numbers in *italics* indicate illustrations

SUGGESTED READING

FAGER, CHARLES. *Selma, 1965: The March That Saved the South.* New York: Charles Scribner's Sons, 1974.

KING, MARTIN LUTHER, JR. *Why We Can't Wait.* New York: Harper & Row, 1964.

RAINES, HOWELL. *My Soul Is Rested: Movement Days in the Deep South Remembered.* New York: G. P. Putnam's Sons, 1977.

SCHULKE, FLIP, ed. *Martin Luther King, Jr.: A Documentary...Montgomery to Memphis.* New York: W. W. Norton & Co., 1976.

WEBB, SHEYANN, and RACHEL WEST NELSON. *Selma, Lord, Selma: Girlhood Memories of the Civil Rights Days.* University, Ala.: University of Alabama Press, 1980.

1 2 3 4 5 6 7 8 9 10—JDL—90 89 88 87 86 85